The Ballad of Osore

Stan Huncilman

May 2022
To Eileen
from
Al French

Copyright © 2022 Stan Huncilman

All rights reserved.

ISBN:978-0-9976197-3-7

DEDICATION

To everyone that buys this book.

ACKNOWLEDGMENTS

Thanks to the inventor(s) of the rhyming dictionary.

THE BALLAD OF OSORE

There once were two fish in the sea

whose only troubles were knowing where to be

for though they mostly gloated

it must be noted

they were known as king and queen of Aqualee.

"Small fish are our dish

yes, we know they are fish

aquatic as we

as any can see

It's simply that we find them most delish, those little fish."

And so for the Kinged and Queened

all was as deemed

Those tiny fishes all

were simply eaten raw

and the tiny's thoughts never gleamed.

Then came a lad

son of king dad

he saw their fate

and started to hate

the idea of a meal of a tad.

"On this I will not subsist

and certainly resist

more than say no

away I will go

and perhaps cease to exist."

"Do not despise

your parents most wise.

Simply do as we do.

Why get in a stew?

Lest we chastise."

With the flap of his tail

away he turned as if with a great press of sail

and said with a huff,

"I'll call your bluff

I shall live in the belly of a whale."

"For there I will be

as a small fish in the sea

food for the large

a bale in barge

till a better life I see."

"And while I'm ingested

and my morals most tested

I'll counsel the beaten

as they are eaten

That their souls will someday be wrested."

"So, to find a whale

to whom I can avail

and live in his belly

though it be smelly

till a better way I unveil."

Down deep he swam

through sea darker than shut clam.

Alone in the current

his quest he soon learnt

was a moral exam.

There at seas' end

his heart started to bend

for nothing he saw

would answer his call

to help him transcend.

Hungry and in dark
he gnawed on salty bark
for he stuck to his vow
that his mouth not allow
fish even if scraps from a shark.

"Oh, is there a whale?
that will hear my tale
or am I destined to float
while the fat fish gloat?
Yet I must for my soul to prevail."

Down on a sandy berm

There wiggled a worm

"You are blocking my hole."

He said to a sole.

"For it's time to my bed squirm."

From the worm's door

was soon heard a snore

"That noise is a rumble

it makes my tummy tumble,"

said the sole as he lay on oceans' ground floor.

His eyes always up
Sole had spied the king's pup
whose journey had tended
to below the water now ended
"Oh, dear is he on me to sup?"

"Here I shall lay
as if made of clay,"
then he heard told
through bubbles not bold
as the strange fish started to say.

"My name is Osore

I'm son of King Nore

Regarding my mother the queen

I'm no more to be seen.

For I've left my home of Aquatorre."

"So why are you here?

And to me wandered so near?

Young fish of such luster

yet lacking royal bluster

Oh, fish from above, 'tis to the bottom you steer!"

"I'm seeking a cetacean
who, in I'll live in meditation.
You see, as I no longer eat fish
I seek a new dish
to ward my deprivation."

"Whoever has heard
a fish utter such a word?
You're fish in fret
a flopper in a moral net.
What could be more absurd?"

"Be that as it may
I'll take time to say
there is an old whale
with tattered tail
that lives not far away."

"This whale that I mention
is most full of good intention
you see he often sets to ink
what he has put himself to think.
No doubt he will end your apprehension."

"If you want to make your goal last

go east to end your fast.

His name is Notal

and his knowledge is total.

Seek and know how your dilemma is cast."

Across current and bar

Osore did spar

till at last he did meet

the spouter he sought to seek

asleep with his mouth ajar.

"Inside I will peek

for the wisdom I seek

for how will he know

If I dally in his below

quiet and most meek."

"Perhaps I can portend

leviathan's wisdoms wend

then sally away

content with my intellectual hay

a heart's quest kenned."

Then snapped a shadow
that capped what was outgo
"Oh, dear I am trapped
for I thought my host napped
Alas I'm locked in his grotto."

Alas it was utter dark
and fluids did mark
where life did end
and to digestion did send.
'Twas not a mendicant's ark.

"If I am to escape
I'd best not hesitate
I entered to be wiser
yet instead will be fertilizer
if a gape is not in my fate."

On fins he crawled
till on nostrils' ports gnawed
soon came a rumble
as the cetacean in nap fumbled
and coughed out Osore awed.

He turned to the whale
so that his quest it did not curtail
"I sought you for wisdom
so entered your innards of doom
but found it not to avail."

"Notal, I'm told you are wise
and most certainly well apprised.
I find my flesh grumbles
if fish into my belly tumbles
I fear I'm a cannibal in disguise."

"I suffer discontent
when I think of nourishment
You being scribe
I'm told can me describe
a diet most content."

"Oh! from my belly has tumbled
a piscine drama most jumbled
what you seek to excise
is a dilemma for the most wise
yet upon an old whale you stumbled."

23

"So, you me deny
and wish me to fly.
Is the wisdom sought
all for naught
or is it a lie I espy?"

"If I were to be
That, that you wish to see
why did you tickle
when locked in my tummy's pickle?
Was it not to your pree?"

24

"I'm a fish in doubt
seeking a redoubt
and you a creature of size
must be uncommonly wise
both inside and out."

"Lacking of advice
and beholden to wisdom's price
I entered your abode
seeking knowledge roed
yet perhaps it was simply not nice."

Slowly the whale responded,
"I see now we are corresponded
for your frantic search
put you in a lurch
for to an answer you are bonded."

"Most certainly so
alas no farther I'll go.
Though my gut is but string
my resolve is no fling.
'Tis starvation unless I know."

"Note that my rations are flailed
not preferred but only that availed.
Or rather I have eaten
anything my teeth have beaten
unconcerned from whence it sailed."

"I have naught
for what you have sought
perhaps others are wise
so journey on I advise
Foolish fish self-fraught."

Being a body near naught

by the current he was caught

down was the motion

into the darkest of ocean

until by bottom forwrought.

"On bottomless mud I'm perched

for in vain I searched

to live in perfection

by holding all others as my reflection

yet into muck I now lurch."

So alas it came to be

his end he could see

his flesh into bones

and bones soon to stones

because of sought purity.

Now our tale cedes tension,

for gone are his noble intentions.

He sought to separate

his world from others incarnate,

by not understanding *thou art that* is more than convention.

ABOUT THE AUTHOR

Sculptor, dog lover and adventurer Stan Huncilman is also contemplative.

Made in the USA
Las Vegas, NV
08 May 2022

48521633R00021